THE SLEEPY HEAD AND THE THREE WISHES

Ages Group: 3-7 years old

El Viaje Bilingüe Del Dormilón Y Los Tres Deseos Mágicos

Enchanting Bilingual Tales in English-Spanish: Mythical Creatures and Early Philosophy for Emotional Intelligence and Building Strong Values

Angelica. Rockford.

The sleepyhead and the three wishes/*El Viaje Bilingüe Del Dormilón Y Los Tres Deseos Mágicos:* Enchanting Bilingual Tales in English-Spanish: Mythical Creatures and Early Philosophy for Emotional Intelligence and Building Strong Values

© Copyright 2023 of First Publication by Angelica Rockford—All right reserved.

Illustrations copyright © 2023 of First Publication by Angelica Rockford. —All rights reserved.

The content contained within this book may not be reproduced, duplicated, or transmitted without direct written permission from the author or the publisher.

The history: Under no circumstances will any blame or legal responsibility be held against the publisher, or author, for any damages, reparation, or monetary loss due to the information contained within this book. Either directly or indirectly. You are responsible for your own choices, actions, and results.

Legal Notice:

This book is copyright protected. This book is only for personal use. You cannot amend, distribute, sell, use, quote, or paraphrase any part, or the content within this book, without the consent of the author or publisher.

Illustration: No part of this publication may be reproduced, stored in a retrieval system, or transmitted, in any form or by any means, electronic, mechanical, photocopying, recording, or otherwise, without the prior written permission of the copyright owner.

Published by Publisher: Angelica Rockford

Publisher's Address: infosunkullay@gmail.com

Publisher's Channels: @angelicarockford @sunkullaybooks

Disclaimer Notice:

Please note the information contained within this document is for educational and entertainment purposes only. All effort has been executed to present accurate, up-to-date, and reliable, complete information. No warranties of any kind are declared or implied. Readers acknowledge that the author is not engaging in the rendering of legal, financial, medical, or professional advice. The content within this book has been derived from various sources. Please consult a licensed professional before attempting any techniques outlined in this book.

By reading this document, the reader agrees that under no circumstances is the author responsible for any losses, direct or indirect, which are incurred as a result of the use of the information contained within this document, including, but not limited to, — errors, omissions, or inaccuracies.

Disclaimer Illustration:

While the author has made every effort to provide accurate historical information, some details may have been simplified, altered, or fictionalized from the imagination of the author for the purpose of storytelling.

The characters and events portrayed in this book are fictitious. Any similarity to real persons, living or dead, is coincidental and not intended by the author.

"The Power of Unity, in a world, that needs it" _ A. Rockford

Whimsical Journeys of Friendship

Dive into "Magical Mischief and Marvels. A bilingual—English and Spanish Chapter Book for Kids Ages 3 to 7. — It is a Laughter-filled adventurous journey where enchanting tales and funny magic come alive, teaching valuable lessons about diversity, empathy, inclusivity, love, forgiveness, and emotional intelligence through the playful lens of spirituality and philosophy that will transform the lives of your children in a magical way that you can't imagine. Offer more than toys. Offer a journey. A journey where:

- Friendship is as easy as a smile.
- Respect isn't taught, it's felt.
- Inner battles fade, and self-love shines.

✸ when parents heal and embrace their self-worth, children naturally flourish. If we address the root — our own self-image and value — we inherently uplift the next generation.

✸ Give lessons, connection, and emotional growth.

A tale designed for the well-being of both parent and child, fostering deep bonds, shared wisdom, and nurturing their inner journey. —What are you waiting for? Open your book, and let the magic begin!

TABLE OF CONTENTS

Connect with Ease.... Little Journeys to Big Friendships.

INTRODUCTION 1
INTRODUCTION OF THE UNBREAKABLE TRIO 5
INTRODUCTION DEL TRÍO IMPARABLE...8

CHAPTER 1
THE SLEEPYHEAD AND THE DARING DUO..11
CAPÍTULO 1
EL DORMILÓN Y EL DÚO ATREVIDO...12
CHAPTER 2
THE SILLY START...14
CAPÍTULO 2
EL TONTO COMIENZO 18
CHAPTER 3
THE ENCHANTED FOREST - MEETING ELYTA THE PEPPY ELF...................... 22

CAPÍTULO 3

EL BOSQUE ENCANTADO - ENCUENTRO CON ELYTA, LA ALEGRE ELFA .24

CHAPTER 4

THE WONDROUS DESERT AND A GENIE'S THREE WISHES 27

CAPÍTULO 4

EL MARAVILLOSO DESIERTO Y LOS TRES DESEOS DEL GENIO 32

CHAPTER 5

YOGI THE YETI AND THE FROSTY ARM 37

CAPÍTULO 5

EL YETI YOGUI Y EL BRAZO HELADO 41

CHAPTER 6

OVERCOMING OBSTACLES AND THE POWER OF FRIENDSHIP 45

CAPÍTULO 6

LA SUPERACIÓN DE OBSTÁCULOS Y EL PODER DE LA AMISTAD 47

CHAPTER 7

A STOP BACK HOME AND A TIME TO REFLECT 50

CAPÍTULO 7

UNA PARADA EN CASA Y UN TIEMPO PARA REFLEXIONAR 53

CHAPTER 8
THE ISLAND OF RIDDLE-DEE-DOODLE 57

CAPÍTULO 8
LA ISLA DE LAS ADIVINANZAS 59

CHAPTER 9
THE LOST CITY IN THE ANCIENT RUINS 62

CAPÍTULO 9
LA CIUDAD PERDIDA EN LAS RUINAS ANTIGUAS 64

CHAPTER 10
PART TWO: THE MOURNFUL CRY IN THE HIDDEN RUINS 67

CAPÍTULO 10
SEGUNDA PARTE: EL GRITO LÚGUBRE EN LAS RUINAS OCULTAS 70

CHAPTER 11
THE SPARKLE CRYSTAL CAVE 74

CAPÍTULO 11
LA CUEVA DE CRISTAL CENTELLEANTE 76

CHAPTER 12
THE MYSTERIOUS JIGGY HEALING GARDEN 79

CAPÍTULO 12

EL MISTERIOSO JARDÍN CURATIVO DE JIGGY. 82

CHAPTER 13

THE SKY-HIGH KINGDOM OF COOPERATION AND APPRECIATION 86

CAPÍTULO 13

EL REINO CELESTIAL DE LA COOPERACIÓN Y EL APRECIO 88

CHAPTER 14

THE FANTABULOUS FRIENDSHIP FINALE 91

CAPÍTULO 14

EL FANTABULOSO FINAL DE LA AMISTAD 93

AFFIRMATIONS

Enhancing Emotional Development Self-Love 102

Self-Love Affirmations 103

Self-Worth Affirmations 104

Patient Affirmations 105

It Is Ok To Make Mistakes Affirmations 106

Uplifting Affirmations 107

Emotional Growth Affirmations..108

Family-Gratitude Affirmations..109

Confidence Affirmations..110

Self-Compassion Affirmations..111

Living In The Present Affirmations..112

Listening Affirmations..113

Mindfulness Affirmations...114

Controlling Anger And Reacting Better Affirmations.....................115

Emotional Growth Affirmations...116

Kindness Affirmations..117

Children With Special Needs — I Am Not My Body Affirmations....118

New Adventure Affirmations..119

Resilience Affirmations..120

Making Friends Affirmations...121

Forgiveness Affirmations...122

Boundaries Affirmations..123

Emotional Intelligence Affirmations..124

A FULL OF GIFTS

The all-in-one children's book that goes beyond storytelling!

A little friend that speaks to your child's mind and a place where you can connect and laugh sincerely with your child.

Welcome to our bilingual adventure—English and Spanish intertwined in a dance of words. Each page is a cross-cultural journey, inviting children to discover the magic of language. This is a place where stories are told in two languages, and every reader is a bridge between words. It is time to "**Speak Spanish**" and foster your child's language skills, opening up a world of bilingual opportunities.

WHY I DO WHAT I DO

As the author, my mission is to create an unforgettable "Childhood" with memorable moments and connections between parents, educators, librarians, and children. Through stories like this one, we can nurture emotional intelligence and well-being in children by teaching essential life lessons, like the power of friendship, teamwork, the beauty of diversity, overcoming fear, and building resilience, primarily through difficult times. As well as promoting values such as empathy, gratitude, compassion, and forgiveness. This strong foundation and support from us will empower them to confidently stand up for themselves later in life, rather than being held back by fear and seeking only safe spaces. That is the reason.

THE STRATEGY TO TEACH CHILDREN.

When we teach children, it is crucial to balance their education with the preservation of their innate, joyful, and energetic natures. For me personally — essence, purity, and innocence through the years have gotten lost, and I love bringing it back to life again, making the journey more fun and effective through engaging tales like this one. I love creating stories where children can easily relate to characters and see them as role models and can learn how to connect with themselves and others while at the same time enhancing creativity and imagination. We should encourage them to engage with others naturally, without the weight of perfectionism or teaching that we "have it all figured out". After all, we were all children once, and nothing in this world is perfect, including ourselves. Understanding this helps us remain open and empathetic. This balance can help children to be more receptive to learning without feeling overwhelmed while they develop early literacy skills.

Here is just a Fraction of What Awaits Young Readers inside this Book

💡 More Than Just a Story:

This book of mythic animals serves as role models, positively influencing children's behavior through their actions and experiences in the story." It provides priceless life lessons and memories that money can't buy, empowering your child to face adversity with resilience, empathy, and friendship. Not only that, it also teaches the importance of nature and what actions to take to preserve Mother Earth's healthy and the environment.

🌍 Shape a Better Future:

By sharing this children's book about overcoming challenges with your child, you're equipping them with the tools to make the world a better place for themselves and future generations, instilling a solid foundation for personal growth and social harmony.

☀️ Foster Lifelong Values:

This heartwarming tale teaches timeless positive values like teamwork, kindness, and respect for nature, shaping your child into a compassionate, confident, and responsible individual. It's a perfect example of teaching values through engaging imaginative stories like this one. Each chapter shares priceless values and essential life lessons that will nurture and nourish kids' and parents ' well-being.

✦ Unlock Your Child's Imagination:

Ignite your child's curiosity and creativity as they journey through mesmerizing landscapes in this kids' story about exploring magical lands and meeting captivating creatures that will spark their imagination and keep them hooked from start to finish.

EXTRA BONUSES

But that's not all! I've packed this book with incredible gifts and unique features to enrich your child's **development and increase their emotional intelligence with our extra bonus of:**

1. **More friends, including himself/herself.** (*Self-Love Affirmations*)
2. **Nurture Confidence and self-imagine.** (*confidence affirmations*)
3. 3. **Being grateful for having you and appreciating all things you do for her/him** (*Gratitude Affirmations*)
4. 4. **Calming their overwhelming feelings or stress by Living in the Present, additionally promoting focus, relaxation, and emotional well-being.** (*Mindfulness*)

This book is a little friend to revisit often.

Algo de español?

English and Spanish Time

"Please, Meet the Unbreakable Trio"

"The grand adventure where everyone's invited."

Once upon a time, in a beautiful world where everyone were friends, but sometimes didn't get along, there lived three extraordinary amigos from very diverse backgrounds; they were known to everyone as "the unbreakable trio."

Pollo—The sleepyhead

Pollo, the sleepy head & the latecomer, is a 6-year-old boy whose ancestral background included **Ukrainians, Serbians, Lithuanians, and Romanians**. He had a peculiar habit of dozing off just about anywhere and arriving late everywhere - on the swings, during hide and seek, and even while eating ice cream! But the curious thing is that he has a natural gift because he likes to forgive; for him, "Forgiveness is a gift of peace."

Katta—The Adventurous Girl

Katta, mostly known as a bossy little girl, **is a stunning 7-year-old girl of Latin, Turkish, and Syrian mixed roots: not to mention that her ancestors also included Palestine and Israel.** with light brown skin who styled her hair into two playful buns.

Katta is a true adventurer girl, always ready to explore the unknown mystery. Climbing the tallest trees, outsmarting the sneakiest foxes, and even finding her way through the darkest caves, she never had a problem pushing fear out of the way. Katta is a strong, resilient, and wild girl, someone you would love to have as your friend. She doesn't know of adversaries because she always had a way of turning foes into allies.

Marto —The Supportive Friend

Marto is an 8-year-old boy from the USA with bouncy afro-textured hair that seemed to dance with joy. Marto is known at school as a quiet kid who rarely speaks, and that might be true, but when he is with his friends at kindergarten and in trouble, he talks non-stop until he's out of breath. He possesses an unstoppable superpower! He can turn any catastrophic situation into a fun adventure. His trick is "living in the present." He is the cheerful one in the group, with his big, calm, contagious smile and huge heart that keeps the group balanced. Whenever his comrades are fighting like cats and dogs, he'll give them a moment of Zen or Buddha, and poof - problem solved! His abilities could make even the wiggliest of worms stand up straight!

Por favor, conozcan al Trío Imparable"

"La gran aventura donde todos están invitados."

Érase una vez, en un hermoso mundo donde todos eran amiguitos, pero a veces no se llevaban bien; ahi vivían tres extraordinarios amigos de orígenes muy diversos; todos los conocían como "el trío imparable"."

Pollo, el Dormilón y el Tardon.

Pollo, el dormilón y el rezagado, es un niño de 6 años cuyos antepasados incluían ucranianos, serbios, lituanos y rumanos. Tenía la peculiar costumbre de quedarse dormido en cualquier sitio y de llegar tarde a todas partes: a los columpios, al escondite e incluso a comer helado. Pero, lo curioso era que, Pollo tenía un don y una medalla de oro, que decía "El perdón es un regalo de paz". Ya que, a Pollo le gustaba perdonar. Por eso siempre llevaba su premio-trofeo de oro a todas partes, incluso para usarla con sus propios amigos, por su propia paz.

Katta, la Aventurera

Katta, conocida sobre todo como una niña mandona, es una despampanante niña de 7 años de raíces mixtas latinas, turcas y sirias, y de piel morena clara que se peina en dos juguetones moños.

Katta es una auténtica aventurera, siempre dispuesta a explorar el misterio desconocido. Trepa a los árboles más altos, es más astuta que los zorros más sabios, e incluso encuentra el camino a través de las cuevas más oscuras. Katta nunca ha tenido problemas para apartar el miedo de su camino. Ella es una chica fuerte, resiliente y salvaje; alguien a quien te encantaría tener como amiga. Pues ella, no conoce de adversarios, solo de aliados.

Marto -El amigo Solidario

Marto es un niño estadounidense de 8 años con una melena de textura afro que parece bailar de alegría. Marto es conocido en el colegio como un niño callado que rara vez habla, y puede que sea cierto, pero cuando está con sus amigos de la guardería y se mete en líos, habla sin parar hasta quedarse sin aliento. Posee un superpoder imparable. Es capaz de convertir cualquier situación catastrófica en una divertida aventura. Su truco es "vivir el presente". Es el alegre del grupo, con su gran sonrisa tranquila y contagiosa y su enorme corazón que mantiene al grupo equilibrado. Cuando sus compañeros se pelean como perros y gatos, él les regala un momento de Zen o de Buda, y zas, ¡problema resuelto! Sus habilidades harían que hasta el gusano más torpe se pusiera erguido.

CHAPTER 1

THE SLEEPYHEAD AND THE DARING DUO

In a cozy village, tucked between rolling hills, lived a daring girl named Katta and her two best pals, Marto and Pollo. Pollo was the Sleepiest Sleepyhead in Sleepy Town - always yawning and late for every adventure. But Katta and Marto were pros at keeping him awake with crazy tricks and surprises. They were an odd trio, but their love for wild escapades glued them together like peanut butter and jelly...

CAPÍTULO 1

EL DORMILÓN Y EL DÚO ATREVIDO

En un acogedor pueblo, escondido entre ondulantes colinas, vivían una atrevida niña llamada Katta y sus dos mejores amigos, Marto y Pollo. Pollo era el dormilón más dormilón del pueblo: siempre bostezaba y llegaba tarde a todas las aventuras. Pero Katta y Marto eran profesionales en mantenerlo despierto con locos trucos y sorpresas. Eran un trío extraño, pero su amor por las aventuras salvajes los unía como la mantequilla de cacahuete y la gelatina...

CHAPTER 2

THE SILLY START

One sunny day, the three amigos were to set off on an epic quest to a magical land bursting with wonder. But they had to tackle one little problem first. Pollo's snooze-button habit. They told him they'd arrive at his house an hour early, knowing he'd be sleeping again. And when they came, they were proven right.

"Oh no, not again!" exclaimed Katta as she entered Pollo's room. They expected to find him sleeping, which he was. What they didn't expect is that he'd be sleeping with his pajamas on backward! It was so silly even his own pajama buttons seemed to laugh at him.

"Wakey wakey Pollo!" they woke him up.
Pollo groggily began to wake.

"Wha-what-what?!" he blurted out, confused about what was happening. His buddies couldn't help but laugh harder.

"Oh, Pollo," they exclaimed, "you've got your pajamas on backward!" With a giggle, they pointed out his backward outfit. They could see their beloved friend was still half-lost in sleep. They'd have to press him to get him up.

"Let's go, little Mr. Pollo, an amazing day awaits us!" said Marto.
"What time is it?" responded Pollo, still half awake.

"It's 7 am!" exclaimed Katta, already anxious to start his day.
"What!?" Pollo quickly shot out of bed.

"Hey! You said it would be at 8 am not 7 am! You lied to me! How could you!" Pollo stood up, grumpy that he'd been woken from bed earlier than promised.

"We knew if we told you to get up at 8 am you'd only be ready by 9 am, and that's too late, so we got here an hour early. Now put your clothes on and get dressed," commanded Katta impatiently.

"Whatever, you lied to me," said Pollo, crossing his arms and comically frowning his face.

"Sometimes I think we know you better than you know yourself," responded Marto, with an understanding look on his face.

"Pollo, get out of those backward pajamas and get dressed," commanded Katta again.

"Post haste Pollo, let's go!" Marto declared. Katta joined him in prodding Pollo to get ready.

Finally, an hour later at (as Marto and Katta predicted), they were entering the forest 's door, which surrounded their small town. But Pollo was still there, fixing his clothes, in a very lazy way, without wanting to move.

As Marto and Katta began to move deeper into the forest, their human energies seemed to awaken the mysterious forest, jolting even the dormant plants and putting them into a vibrant state of alertness.

Pollo, still half asleep an hour after waking, realized he was beginning to fall behind his friends. "Ah? —Hey! Guys, wait for me! Stop walking so fast!".

In a flurry of hurried movement, he swiftly tucked in his loose shirt and hurried forward to reach his friends.

"There he is!" giggled Marto. "We thought we lost you!".

"Woo hoo!!" shouted Katta suddenly with a burst of joy, leaping into the air, stretching her arms wide open.

"Hooray!" exclaimed Marto and Pollo in unison, joining Katta.

The three friends continued to march into the forest, excited for the adventures the coming day was sure to bring.

All kids have a powerful hero and a magic princess inside them.

CAPÍTULO 2

EL TONTO COMIENZO

Un día soleado, los tres amigos iban a emprender una búsqueda épica hacia una tierra mágica llena de maravillas. Pero antes tenían que resolver un pequeño problema. El hábito de Pollo de quedarse dormido. Le dijeron que llegarían a su casa una hora antes, sabiendo que volvería a dormir. Y cuando llegaron, les dieron la razón.

"¡Hay noooo, otra vez no!", exclamó Katta al entrar en la habitación de Pollo.

Esperaban encontrarlo durmiendo, y así lo era. ¡Lo que no esperaban es que estuviera durmiendo con el pijama al revés! Era tan tonto que hasta los botones de su pijama parecían reírse de él.

"¡Despierta, despierta Pollo!", Le despertaron.

Pollo empezó a despertarse.

"¡¿Qu-qué-qué?!" soltó, confundido por lo que estaba pasando. Sus compañeros no pudieron evitar reírse más.

"Oh, Pollo", exclamaron, "¡tienes el pijama al revés!". Con una risita, le señalaron su atuendo al revés. Podían ver que su querido amigo seguía medio dormido. Tendrían que presionarle para que se levantara.

"¡Vamos, pequeño señor Pollo, nos espera un día increíble!", dijo Marto.

"¿Qué hora es?" respondió Pollo, aún medio despierto.

"¡Son las 7 de la mañana!", exclamó Katta, ya ansioso por empezar el día.

"¿Qué?" Pollo salió disparado de la cama.

"¡Hey! ¡Dijiste que sería a las 8 am no a las 7 am! ¡Me has mentido! ¿Cómo se atrevieron? Pollo se levantó, malhumorado por haber sido despertado de la cama antes de lo prometido.

"Sabíamos que si te decíamos que te levantaras a las 8 am sólo estarías listo a las 9 am, y eso es demasiado tarde, así que llegamos una hora antes. Ahora ponte la ropa y vístete!", le ordenó Katta, impaciente.

"Da igual, me han mentido", dijo Pollo, cruzándose de brazos y frunciendo cómicamente el ceño.

"A veces creo que te conocemos mejor que tú mismo", respondió Marto, con cara de comprensión.

"Pollo, quítate ese pijama atrasado y vístete", ordenó Katta de nuevo.

"¡Date prisa Pollo, vamonos!" declaró Marto. Katta se unió a él para incitar a Pollo a prepararse.

Por fin, una hora más tarde (como Marto y Katta habían predicho), salian por la puerta del bosque que rodeaba su pequeña ciudad. Pero Pollo seguía allí, arreglándose la ropa, de una manera muy vaga, sin querer moverse.

Cuando Marto y Katta empezaron a adentrarse en el bosque, sus energias humanas parecian desper el bosque, sacudiendo incluso a las plantas más dormilonas, y ponerlos en un vibrante estado de alerta.

Pollo, todavía medio dormido una hora después de despertarse, se dio cuenta de que empezaba a quedarse atras con respecto a sus amigos. "¿Ah? -¡Eh! ¡Chicos, esperadme! Dejad de andar tan deprisa!".

En una ráfaga de movimientos apresurados, se acomodó rápidamente la camisa suelta y se apresuró a avanzar para alcanzar a sus amigos.

"¡Ahí está!", rió Marto.

"¡Pensábamos que te habíamos perdido!".

"¡¡¡yo hoo!!!", gritó de repente Katta con un estallido de alegría, saltando en el aire y estirando los brazos de par en par.

"¡Hurra!", exclamaron Marto y Pollo juntos, uniéndose a Katta.

Los tres amigos continuaron su marcha hacia el bosque, entusiasmados por las aventuras que seguro les depararía el día siguiente.

CHAPTER 3

THE ENCHANTED FOREST - MEETING ELYTA THE PEPPY ELF

Their journey through the thick forest eventually brought them into the company of Elyta, a peppy elf, who showed them around through the wild woods.

She introduced the trio to a rare variety of moving plants with leaves that trembled like the mean kids at kindergarten, who would say "Don't touch me!" when you tried to be nice to them.

She also showed them peculiar animals of all shapes, sizes, and smells. Some smelled like roses, and others stank like Katta's farts! Suddenly, they spotted a beautiful colored unicorn nibbling grass that represented union- all the colors of children and listened to fairies strumming their tiny fairy instruments.

At a certain point, the trio and their new elf friend Elyta stopped and sat under a tree to take a rest. To tease Pollo, his friends trick him, making him believe they'd reached the end of the road, only to reveal they were still halfway on the road. —Oh no! ... Sure, their buddies fibbed a bit, but Pollo's ready to let bygones be bygones! because he always wore his gold medal with him, which said, "Forgiveness is a gift of peace..." After all, it's the thought that counts, right? Onward, Team Unstoppable!" Katta and Marto never judged their buddy 's naptime adventures.! Nope, They love him exactly as he was —"a sleepyhead, the world-class snooze champion, where giggles with him were a gift!

CAPÍTULO 3

EL BOSQUE ENCANTADO - ENCUENTRO CON ELYTA, LA ALEGRE ELFA

Su viaje a través del espeso bosque les llevó finalmente a la compañía de Elyta, una alegre elfa, que les mostró los alrededores del bosque salvaje.

Ella presentó al trío una rara variedad de plantas móviles, con hojas que temblaban como las niñas fresas del Jardín, que decían "¡No me toques!" cuando intentabas ser amable con ellas.

También les mostró animales peculiares de todas las formas, tamaños y olores. Algunos olían a rosas y otros apestaban como los pedos de Katta. De repente, vieron un hermoso unicornio de colores mordisqueando la hierba que representaba la unión: todos los colores de los niños, y escucharon a las hadas rasguear sus diminutos instrumentos de hadas.

En un momento dado, el trío y su nueva amiga elfa Elyta se detuvieron y se sentaron bajo un árbol a descansar.

Para burlarse de Pollo, sus amigos lo engañaron, haciéndole creer que habían llegado al final del camino, sólo para revelarle que aún estaban a mitad de camino. -¡Oh no! Pobre Pollo, sus amigos le han mentido un poco, pero Pollo está dispuesto a olvidar el pasado, porque siempre llevaba su medalla de oro a todas partes, que decía,"el perdón es un regalo de paz entre amigos..."Después de todo, lo que cuenta es la intención, ¿verdad? ¡Es mas! Equipo Imparable!"

Katta y Marto nunca juzgaron las aventuras de su amigo a la hora de la siesta. No, le querían tal y como era: "un dormilón, el campeón mundial de la siesta, donde reirse con el, era un regalo.

CHAPTER 4

THE WONDROUS DESERT AND A GENIE'S THREE WISHES

"Repetition is key to teach kids. "A. Rockford.

After emerging from the forest and traveling for some time, they eventually found themselves venturing into a vast desert, where they met a tiny genie named, well, Genie. Genie granted them each three wishes to help humanity. Genie reminded them of the importance of choosing their wishes wisely, then disappeared.

Katta was quick to make her first wish. She wished for "peace, union, and empathy."

Next was Marto, who wished for "self-acceptance, self-love, and self-healing."

The last to make a wish was Pollo, who decided to say his desire out loud. He wished for "never-ending ice cream, cakes, biscuits, and Lolli…" – he was quickly cut off mid-wish by Katta.

"No, Pollo, wait!" she exclaimed. His friends couldn't help but facepalm and chuckle. "That's not what the wishes are for," said Katta. "Remember what Genie said - ask for something powerful and generous for humanity that can help all the world".

"Like what?!" asked Pollo, confused.

"Like forgiveness, good feelings… I don't know… but not sweets!!" Katta continued, this time trying hard to be empathetic and not judge her buddy.

A look of understanding seemed to fall upon Pollo's face. "Oh, ok, ok, I see now! I wish for understanding, forgiveness, and respect among all people." Pollo paused momentarily. "And never-ending ice cream".

"No, Pollo! You only have three wishes! Why is this so hard for you to understand!" shouted Katta, now clearly losing her patience. Katta wanted to push her friend, but she reminded herself that Pollo was her good friend.

Her mother taught her that whenever she was angry and felt like lashing out, she should say to herself: "I am feeling angry right now, and I need space to recover my superpowers and find ways to feel better!"

In the midst of trying to calm herself, Katta was interrupted by Pollo's crying. "Waaa!!!". Pollo's outcry took her by surprise, his small face scrunching up as the tears came pouring down.

Then, Pollo's crying triggered Katta, who began crying too! Seeing her friend so upset made her tiny heart feel a little bit bad inside.

"¡¡¡Waaa!!!". Now, they were both crying.

Marto, upon seeing them, covered his ears so he wouldn't hear their loud shrieks that seemed to wake up the invisible birds that were napping in the enchanted desert.

"I wish for Katta to not be mean anymore… and to never stink!. Waaaa!!" He hiccupped out each word, interrupted by a sniffle and a sob, his tiny fists clenched tightly in his frustration and sorrow.

Marto laughed out loud at Pollo's unusual wish.

Katta's tears evaporated almost as quickly as they had appeared, swept away by her friend's words. But in a surprising twist, her mood changed back to irritation. Her brow furrowed, and a huff escaped her lips, revealing a tiny tempest of frustration brewing within.

Marto noticed Katta's mood shift and jumped in to de-escalate the situation. "It's ok, guys, let's not fight. We're friends. We are on a new adventure, exploring and discovering beautiful things. This is an adventure, a new discovery, a new experience to GROW as heroes - not as rivals. So let 's focus on the beautiful present! And presently, we are in the heart of this magical desert, with the sun kindly smiling on us." Said Marto, his voice soothing a reflection on the mind of Pollo and Katta.

Marto was the calm one, always able to diffuse any situation among the three and save the day.

Both Katta and Pollo reflected immediately, then looked at each other eye-to-eye, and their hearts were reunited again as friends.

"Sorry for losing my temper, Pollo, I didn't mean it." Katta expressed sincerely.

"Me too, but please respect my boundaries. Boundaries protect my emotions, and I have the right to say "NO." "I am kind to you, and you will be nice to me, ok?" Pollo responded assertively with a sparkle in his eyes, extending his arms to gently wrap Katta in a heartfelt, teddy bear-tight hug, which she returned.

A genuine pact of forgiveness sealed in their innocent embrace. Letting go of the past and starting fresh in the present.

Marto, now feeling left out, joined in for a group hug, and the trio began laughing. "Yes, let's be kind to each other" Exclaimed Marto, hugging them even more.

Also, Katta understood that day: Boundaries protect our emotions, and everyone had the right to say "NO," including herself. So, she was ready to respect her buddy's boundaries in forward _ Well, at least she would try."

CAPÍTULO 4

El Maravilloso Desierto y los Tres Deseos del Genio

Después de salir del bosque y viajar durante algún tiempo, finalmente se aventuraron en un vasto desierto, donde conocieron a un pequeño genio llamado, bueno, Genio.

Genio les concedió tres deseos para ayudar a la humanidad. Genio les recordó la importancia de elegir bien sus deseos y luego desapareció.

Katta se apresuró a pedir su primer deseo. Deseó "paz, unión y empatía".

La siguiente fue Marto, que deseó "aceptarse uno mismo, amor propio y autocuración".

El último en pedir un deseo fue Pollo, que decidió decirlo en voz alta. Deseó "helados, pasteles, chupetines y muchos chicles encaramelados...", pero Katta le interrumpió a mitad del deseo.

"¡No, Pollo, espera!", exclamó. Sus amigos no pudieron evitar una mueca y una risita.

"Los deseos no son para eso", dijo Katta. "Recuerda lo que dijo Genio: pide algo poderoso y generoso para la humanidad que pueda ayudar a todo el mundo".

"¡¿Como qué?!" preguntó Pollo, confundido.

"Como perdón, buenos sentimientos... no sé... ¡¡¡pero no dulces!!!". Continuó Katta, esta vez esforzándose por ser paciente y no juzgar a su compañero.

Una mirada de comprensión pareció caer sobre el rostro de Pollo. "Oh, vale, vale, ¡ahora lo entiendo! Deseo comprensión, perdón y respeto entre todas las personas". Pollo hizo una pausa momentánea. "Y muchos chupetines, tambien".

"¡No, Pollo! ¡Sólo tienes tres deseos! ¿Por qué te cuesta tanto entenderlo?", gritó Katta, que estaba perdiendo la paciencia. Katta quería empujar a su amigo, pero se recordó a sí misma que Pollo era su buen amigo. Su madre le enseñó que siempre que estuviera enfadada y tuviera ganas de pelear, debía decirse a sí misma: "¡Ahora mismo estoy enfadada y necesito espacio para recuperar mis superpoderes y encontrar la manera de sentirme mejor!".

En medio de su intento por calmarse, Katta fue interrumpida por el llanto de Pollo. "¡¡¡Waaa!!!". El grito de Pollo la tomó por sorpresa, su pequeño rostro se arrugó mientras las lágrimas caían a raudales.

Entonces, el llanto de Pollo provocó a Katta, ¡que empezó a llorar también! Ver a su amiga tan disgustada hizo que su pequeño corazón se sintiera un poco mal por dentro.

"¡¡¡Waaa!!!". Ahora ambos estaban llorando. Marto, al verlos, sólo se tapó los oídos para no oír sus chillidos que parecían despertar a los pájaros invisibles que dormían la siesta en el desierto encantado.

"Deseo que Katta no sea mandona... ¡y que nunca apeste más!." Waaaa!!!"

Soltaba cada palabra con hipo, interrumpido por un resoplido y un sollozo, con sus diminutos puños cerrados con fuerza por su frustración y pena.

Marto rió a carcajadas ante el insólito deseo de Pollo.

Las lágrimas de Katta se evaporaron casi tan rápido como habían aparecido, arrastradas por las palabras de su amiga. Pero en un giro sorprendente, su humor volvió a la irritación. Su ceño se frunció y un resoplido escapó de sus labios, revelando una pequeña tempestad de frustración que se estaba gestando en su interior.

Marto se dio cuenta del cambio de humor de Katta e intervino para calmar la situación. "Está bien, chicos, no nos peleemos. Somos amigos. Estamos en una nueva aventura, aprendiendo y explorando, y esta es una nueva experiencia para CRECER como héroes, no como rivales. ¡Así que concentrémonos en el hermoso presente! Y en el presente, estamos en el corazón de este desierto mágico, con el sol sonriéndonos amablemente". Marto era el tranquilo, siempre capaz de calmar cualquier situación entre los tres y salvar el día.

Tanto Katta como Pollo reflexionaron de inmediato, luego se miraron a los ojos y sus corazones volvieron a reunirse como amigos.

""Siento haber perdido los nervios, Pollo, no era mi intención". expresó Katta con sinceridad.

"Yo también, pero por favor respeta mis límites. Los límites protegen mis emociones, y tengo derecho a decir "NO" "Soy amable contigo, y tú seras amable conmigo, de acuerdo?"" Pollo respondió asertivamente, extendiendo los brazos para envolver suavemente a Katta en un sentido y apretado abrazo de osito de peluche, que ella devolvió. Un auténtico pacto de perdón fue sellado en su inocente abrazo. Dejaron atrás el pasado y empezaron de cero en el presente.

Marto, que ahora se sentía excluido, se unió al abrazo y el trío empezó a reír. "Sí, seamos amables los unos con los otros" respondió Marto abrazándolos aún más.

Además, Katta comprendió ese día, que los límites protegen tus emociones, y todo el mundo tiene derecho a decir "NO", incluida ella misma. Así que se estaba lista en respetar los límites de su amigo". – Bueno, al menos lo intentaria.

CHAPTER 5

YOGI THE YETI AND THE FROSTY ARM

Having left the desert to continue on their journey, their final stop was a snow-covered mountain, where they met a friendly Yeti named Yogi. To their surprise, Yogi had only a single arm, just like Marto!

A wonderful bond between Marto and Yogi formed in that single instant as if a magical thread had woven their hearts together.

Marto felt an immediate kinship with the giant Yogi in a way he'd never known before. It was his first-time meeting someone as formidable as Yogi, who also had just a single arm. Yogi the Yeti also felt the same way, as if he had found a brother, a family he never had.

Pollo and Katta could also sense Mato and Yogi's astonishing bond of unity and were just as surprised as Marto to realize that even powerful creatures could be missing an arm.

Yeti was very excited to teach them all the secrets of all of his powers; he started by revealing his secrets of snowman wizardry, teaching them how to build a snowman, and leading them on a thrilling sledding adventure down a hill. He also revealed to the three amigos his trick to staying confident, which to him was "smiling, being kind with others and himself, and believing he could do the right thing."

"That's it?" questioned Marto.

"That is what confidence looks like for me," Yogi confirmed.

"What makes you smile, Yeti? Asked Katta

"What makes me smile is seeing children laugh because all kids in the world are a GIFT of happiness. _ Our happiness, the happiness of the world; and there is not an EXCEPTION." Said the Yeti, smiling." - And know that you are loved and important for just breathing and don't have to do anything to be loved. " Continued Yeti saying...

"Mom said that too; every child on this planet is beautiful and has something unique to offer the world," Marto replied.

"That's right, my dear little friend," Yeti replied.

"Yeti, we brought you a smile as a Christmas present or for when you need it," said Pollo with a twinkle in his eye.

"And many hugs as well," said Katta

"Oh...thank you for thinking of me; you made my day," thanked Yeti, blushing.

Enchanted with their new friendship. Marto felt inspired to create a snowy gift for Yogi: a GIANT, FROSTY ARM as an expression of gratitude. Seeing Marto's courage and effort, his buddies thought about how Marto sometimes wished to have two arms.

Their friends, with kind and empathetic smiles, asked, "Hey Marto, that snow arm looks fantastic! Can we help you finish it?" Marto's face lit up with a grateful smile, and he nodded in agreement.

Together, they built a brilliant snow arm for Yogi and then another for Marto, too!

Yogi's heart swelled with joy by their thoughtful gift. And he started to cry like a baby, but in happiness.

That afternoon, they continued to share smiles and stories until the day wound down to a close. They learned about the Yeti's unique culture and how his kind lived in harmony with nature and with the animals, and Yogi suggested them to live the same way (internally and externally) with other children their age.

The three friends agreed, and the group parted ways with Yogi with a hug. It was time for them to continue on their journey.

CAPÍTULO 5

EL YETI YOGUI Y EL BRAZO HELADO

Tras abandonar el desierto para continuar su viaje, su última parada fue una montaña nevada, donde conocieron a un simpático Yeti llamado Yogi. Para su sorpresa, Yogi sólo tenía un brazo, ¡igual que Marto!

En ese instante se formó un vínculo maravilloso entre Marto y Yogui, como si un hilo mágico hubiera entretejido sus corazones. Marto sintió de inmediato un parentesco con el gigante Yogui como nunca antes había sentido. Era la primera vez que conocía a alguien tan formidable como Yogui, que además tenía un solo brazo. Yogui el Yeti también sintió lo mismo, como si hubiera encontrado un hermano, una familia que nunca tuvo. Pollo y Katta también podían sentir el asombroso lazo de unidad de Mato y Yogi, y estaban tan sorprendidos como Marto al darse cuenta de que incluso a criaturas poderosas les podía faltar un brazo.

El Yeti estaba muy emocionado por enseñarles los secretos de todos sus poderes, empezó por revelarles sus secretos de hechicero de muñecos de nieve, enseñándoles a construir un muñeco de nieve y guiándoles en una emocionante aventura en trineo colina abajo. También reveló a los tres amigos su truco para mantener la confianza en sí mismo, que para él consistía en "sonreír, ser amable con los demás y consigo mismo, y creer que podía hacer lo correcto".

"¿Eso es todo?", preguntó Marto.

"Así es la confianza para mí", confirmó Yogui.

"¿Qué te hace sonreír, Yeti? preguntó Katta

"Lo que me hace sonreír, es ver reír a los niños, porque todos los niños del mundo son un REGALO de felicidad. Nuestra felicidad, la felicidad del mundo; y no hay una EXCEPCIÓN. " Dijo el yeti sonriendo." — Y sabed que, sois queridos e importantes por solo respirar y no tienen que hacer nada para ser amados. " Dijo el yeti sonriendo.

"mama tambien dijo eso, todos los niños de este planeta son hermosos y tienen algo único que ofrecer al mundo." Respondio Marto.

"Asi es, my queridito amiguito" respondio. Yeti

"Yeti, te hemos traído una sonrisa como regalo de Navidad, o para cuando lo necesites" dijo Pollo con un brillo en los ojos.

"Y muchos abrazos también," dijo Katta.

"Oh... gracias por pensar en mí, me habéis alegrado el día" agradeció el Yeti sonrojándose.

Encantado con su nueva amistad. Marto se sintió inspirado para crear un regalo nevado para Yogui: un BRAZO GIGANTE Y HELADO como expresión de gratitud. Al ver la valentía y el esfuerzo de Marto', sus amigos pensaron que a veces Marto deseaba tener dos brazos.

Sus amigos, con sonrisas amables y empáticas, preguntaron: "¡Eh, Marto, ese brazo de nieve tiene una pinta fantástica! Podemos ayudarte a terminarlo?". A Marto' se le iluminó la cara con una sonrisa de agradecimiento y asintió con la cabeza.

Juntos construyeron un brillante brazo de nieve para Yogui y luego otro para Marto.

A Yogui se le hinchó el corazón de alegría por el regalo y se puso a llorar como un niño, pero de felicidad.

Esa tarde siguieron compartiendo sonrisas e historias hasta que el día llegó a su fin. Aprendieron sobre la cultura única del Yeti y cómo los de su especie vivían en armonía con la naturaleza y con los animales, y Yogi sugirió intentar vivir (internamente y afuera) de la misma manera con otros niños de su edad.

Los tres amigos estuvieron de acuerdo, y el grupo se despidió de Yogui con un abrazo. Era hora de que continuaran su viaje.

CHAPTER 6

OVERCOMING OBSTACLES AND THE POWER OF FRIENDSHIP

As they continued on their journey, Katta, Marto, and Pollo faced lots of challenges - like crossing a shaky bridge and sneaking out of a dragon's lair.

But they remembered Yeti's words "All children are a gift to the world and they can do beautiful things together as a team". That gave them more strength and inspired them to look for a solution that would help them and not cause them to feel fear or panic because they knew being afraid would not help them with anything or get them anywhere. They had to have faith in themselves. But the funny thing was, Pollo snoozed a lot even in the challenges, but his pals had his back with funny jokes, goofy dances, and even Katta's super stinky farts to keep him awake! It was only through their combined support of each other that they were able to face and overcome each challenge because Yeti had also said, " All kids always do things RIGHT. They are learning and growing. Therefore, they are allowed to make mistakes—one step at a time." What Yeti meant was that they should be more patient with their dearest friend, Pollo; since he was the smallest of all and found learning difficult, he was still making progress, but he was learning, although slowly but surely.

Together, the friends relied on each other's strengths and faced each challenge head-on. _They were a gift to each other. Marto, a boy who always used to feel lonely, realized that he was no longer feeling lonely. Still, he also understood that sometimes it's okay to play by yourself. After all, we all like to be alone sometimes, but it's also fun to play with friends!"

CAPÍTULO 6

LA SUPERACIÓN DE OBSTÁCULOS Y EL PODER DE LA AMISTAD

A medida que avanzaban en su viaje, Katta, Marto y Pollo se enfrentaron a un montón de retos, como cruzar un puente inestable-colgante y escabullirse de la guarida de un dragón. Pero recordaron las palabras de Yeti "Todos los niños son un regalo para el mundo y pueden hacer cosas maravillosas juntos como equipo". Eso les dio más fuerza y les inspiró a buscar una salida que les ayudara, y a no tener miedo, ni pánico, porque sabían que eso no les ayudaría en nada, ni les llevaría a ninguna lugar. Tenían que tener fe en sí mismos. Pero lo gracioso era que Pollo dormía mucho, incluso en los desafíos, pero sus amigos lo cubrían espaldas con bromas divertidas, bailes graciosos e incluso pedos apestosos de Katta, para mantenerle despierto porque Yeti también les había dicho "Los niños siempre hacen las cosas BIEN. Estan aprendiendo y creciendo, paso a paso, por eso estaban permitidos cometer errores". Lo que quería decir era que debían tener más paciencia con Pollo, su querido amigo; ya que era el más pequeño de todos y le costaba aprender, pero estaba haciendo progreso, aunque lentamente, pero seguro.

 Sólo el apoyo mutuo les permitió enfrentarse a todos los retos y superarlos. Juntos, los amigos se apoyaron en los puntos fuertes de los demás y se enfrentaron a cada reto de frente. _Eran un regalo, el uno para el otro. Marto, un niño que siempre solía sentirse solo, se dio cuenta, de que ya no se sentía solo, pero también comprendió que a veces está bien jugar solo. Al fin y al cabo, a todos nos gusta estar solos a veces, ¡pero también es divertido jugar con amigos!".

CHAPTER 7

A STOP BACK HOME AND A TIME TO REFLECT

The trio began their journey back home. They needed some time to rest and think about their adventures.

"Who's got my back?" shouted Marto suddenly, startling his friends.

"I do!" Katta answered enthusiastically.

"Me too!" Pollo declared with as much energy as he could muster, as he was half asleep.

Pollo suddenly became more alert and loudly asked, "Who's got my back?"

"No one! Because you sleep too much, you silly goose! Hahahah!!" Katta teased.

The trio started laughing together uncontrollably.

"Nasty Katta," said Pollo, causing the trio to laugh even harder.

"We've got your back, Pollo, and you know it," said Marto, able to temporarily stifle his laughter.

"But it is true, you're always tired or sleeping, and you're definitely late for every adventure. If we weren't all bunking together in the same place, able to wake you up, who knows where you'd be?" said Marto.

"But hey! We don't mind," said Katta. "We like having your around for your silly energy". Katta's tone made it clear she had Pollo's back as well.

"My papa used to say, 'You don't have to do anything to be loved. You are loved just because you exist'," Katta continued. "I really miss my dad." They hugged her as it comforted her.

The trio soon arrived home safe, full of gratitude, and filled with magical memories. Marto discovered that family comes in different ways, shapes, and sizes, not necessarily through blood. Friends were also a family. He would never forget his buddy, or, should we call it, his ol' brother — Yogi the Yeti. They promised to keep exploring and learning about the planet. They vowed to continue exploring both the real and the magical world, knowing that even when faced with challenges, they could overcome anything by working together and relying on each other's strengths. They also learned that magic exists all around us, waiting to be discovered by curious and adventurous souls. The power of true friendship.

But first, they needed to get some sleep. Especially Pollo.

CAPÍTULO 7

UNA PARADA EN CASA Y UN TIEMPO PARA REFLEXIONAR

El trío emprendió el viaje de vuelta a casa. Necesitaban tiempo para descansar y pensar en sus aventuras.

"¿Quién me cubre las espaldas?", gritó Marto de repente, sobresaltando a sus amigos.

"¡Yo!" respondió Katta con entusiasmo.

"¡Yo también!" declaró Pollo con toda la energía que pudo reunir, ya que estaba medio dormido.

De repente, Pollo se puso más alerta y preguntó en voz alta: "¿Quién me cubre las espaldas?".

"¡Nadie! ¡Porque duermes demasiado, ganso tonto! Jajajaja!" se burló Katta.

El trío empezó a reír incontrolablemente.

"Katta asqueroso", dijo Pollo, provocando que el trío se riera aún más.

"Te cubrimos las espaldas, Pollo, y lo sabes", dijo Marto, capaz de sofocar temporalmente su risa.

"Pero es verdad, siempre estás cansado o durmiendo, y sin duda llegas tarde a todas las aventuras. Si no estuviéramos todos juntos en la misma litera, capaces de despertarte, quién sabe dónde estarías, hasta los monos magicos te hubiesen comido", dijo Marto.

"¡Pero bueno! No nos importa", dijo Katta. "Nos gusta tenerte cerca por tu energía tonta". El tono de Katta dejaba claro que también apoyaba a Pollo.

"Mi padre solía decir: 'No tienes que hacer nada para que te quieran. Te quieren sólo porque existes'", continuó Katta. "Echo mucho de menos a mi papá". Termino, y sus amiguitos le abrazaron para consolarle.

El trío no tardó en llegar a casa sano y salvo, lleno de gratitud y de mágicos recuerdos. Marto descubrió que la familia se presenta de diferentes maneras, formas y tamaños, no necesariamente a través de la sangre. Y que los amigos tambien eran familia.

Nunca olvidaría a su amigo o, mejor dicho, a su viejo hermano, Yogui el Yeti. Prometieron seguir explorando y aprendiendo sobre el planeta. Prometieron seguir explorando tanto el mundo real como el mágico, sabiendo que, incluso cuando se enfrentaban a retos, podían superarlos trabajando juntos y confiando en los puntos fuertes de cada uno. También aprendieron que la magia existe a nuestro alrededor, esperando a ser descubierta por almas curiosas y aventureras. El poder de la verdadera amistad. Pero antes, necesitaban dormir un poco. Sobre todo Pollo.

CHAPTER 8

THE ISLAND OF RIDDLE-DEE-DOODLE

After a few days of rest, curiosity again tickled their toes, and Katta, Marto, and Pollo decided to sail to a mysterious island they'd heard about. They didn't hesitate for a second to depart to their next adventure — and who could blame them? Their hearts were captivated by the mystery of the unknown. Daring to go where no kid has gone before, with a side of laughter and satisfaction!

Along their journey, they found a jungle paradise filled with plants that danced and sang, and animals that chatted excitedly with each other. The island was jam-packed with riddles, which they solved to discover its secrets, all while making sure Pollo stayed awake with hilarious jokes and pranks. As they continued on, they bumped into a smarty-pants tortoise with a serious case of the "been-there, done-that." This shelled master-know-it-all told them old stories from the island's past and instructed them on how to be planet-friendly buddies to all the species in the jungle and in their own neighborhood.

Pollo, having spent the whole night devouring the island history book, was extremely frustrated that the tortoise knew everything. He had been excited to share with his friends all the facts he'd learned about the island's history to be proudly called by his friends as the know-it-all, but it seems that someone had already taken that place.

CAPÍTULO 8

LA ISLA DE LAS ADIVINANZAS

Tras unos días de descanso, la curiosidad volvió a hacer cosquillas en sus dedos, y Katta, Marto y Pollo decidieron navegar hasta una misteriosa isla de la que habían oído hablar. No dudaron ni un segundo en partir hacia su próxima aventura — ¿y quién podría culparles? Sus corazones estaban cautivados por el misterio de lo desconocido. Se atrevieron a ir donde ningún niño había ido antes, ¡con un toque de risa y satisfacción!

A lo largo de su viaje, encontraron un paraíso selvático lleno de plantas que bailaban y cantaban, y animales que charlaban animadamente entre sí. La isla estaba repleta de acertijos, que resolvieron para descubrir sus secretos, todo mientras se aseguraban de que Pollo se mantuviera despierto con bromas y travesuras divertidísimas. A medida que avanzaban, se toparon con una tortuga sabelotodo con un grave caso de "ya lo he hecho". Este sabelotodo con caparazón les contó viejas historias del pasado de la isla y les instruyó sobre cómo ser compañeros respetuosos con el planeta de todas las especies de la selva y de su propio vecindario.

Pollo, que se había pasado toda la noche devorando el libro de historia de la isla estaba muy frustrado porque la tortuga lo sabía todo. Le había hecho mucha ilusión compartir con sus amigos todos los datos que había aprendido sobre la historia de la isla, Lo había hecho para que sus amigos le llamaran con orgullo el sabelotodo, pero parece que alguien ya le había quitado ese lugar.

CHAPTER 9

THE LOST CITY IN THE ANCIENT RUINS

On their way going wherever their feet felt like taking them, unexpectedly, they found an old map buried in the ground with words so hidden that they were nearly invisible. After a deep cleaning, they were able to make out the directions and decided to follow the map. And guess what? They found the ancient ruins that they'd heard only from the lips of their Papos and Mamas!! The trio excitedly ventured into ancient ruins hidden deep within the forest. Filled with mysterious carvings and hidden chambers, they couldn't help but explore every nook and cranny. As they deciphered the ancient script, they learned about the history and legends of a lost civilization that once thrived on the island, along with the powerful magic that had been forgotten over time. Marto and Katta took turns keeping Pollo engaged by quizzing him on their discoveries. They learned that preserving history and culture is essential for future generations, but they didn't understand completely.

CAPÍTULO 9

LA CIUDAD PERDIDA EN LAS RUINAS ANTIGUAS

En su camino hacia donde sus pies quisieran llevarlos, inesperadamente encontraron un viejo mapa enterrado en el suelo con palabras tan ocultas que eran casi invisibles. Tras una limpieza a fondo, pudieron distinguir las indicaciones y decidieron seguir el mapa. ¿Y adivina qué? Encontraron las antiguas ruinas de las que sólo habían oído hablar a sus papás y mamás.

El trío se aventuró con entusiasmo en las antiguas ruinas ocultas en lo más profundo del bosque. Llenas de misteriosas tallas y cámaras ocultas, no pudieron evitar explorar cada rincón. Mientras descifraban la antigua escritura, aprendieron sobre la historia y las leyendas de una civilización perdida que una vez prosperó en la isla, junto con la poderosa magia que se había olvidado con el tiempo. Marto y Katta se turnaron para mantener ocupado a Pollo interrogándole sobre sus descubrimientos. Aprendieron que preservar la historia y la cultura es esencial para las generaciones futuras, pero no lo entendia de todo.

CHAPTER 10

PART TWO: THE MOURNFUL CRY IN THE HIDDEN RUINS

The night wants to fall, but it can't, just like their bodies want to stop but can't due to their curious brains that are keeping them going.

As they were heading back to their boat to leave the island, they encountered a large cave. Curious as ever, they decided to enter. When inside, they discovered a number of large chambers, all seemingly leading in different directions. To determine which chamber to enter, they played a game of "eeny meeny miny moe". This eventually landed them in the left-most chamber in the cave.

While traveling through the chamber, they discovered an ancient script.

As they attempted to decipher the ancient script, suddenly, they heard a mournful, crying voice. They looked up and down the chamber but saw nothing. Their bodies started to tremble with fear. Pollo's hair stood up, and he, maybe for the first time in his life, suddenly didn't sleep! Marto jumped involuntarily, causing his glasses to pop off his nose and shatter on the cave floor (fortunately, he never left home without a replacement.) "H-e-ll-o, is someone there", Katta called out bravely.

They all paused a moment, but there was no response.

"H-E-E-LL-o-o-o?" Pollo stammered, struggling to articulate the word properly.

"Shhh!!" Katta whispered urgently.

"No, you shhh! Bossy girl," Pollo replied in anger.

"All right, that's enough; you guys are always fighting like cats and dogs," stated Marto impatiently. "I'll walk further ahead to see what I can find out. You two wait here."

Before Pollo and Katta could protest, the cave suddenly became quiet. Too quiet. Even the sound of water dripping down the edge of the cave walls had seemingly stopped.

Total silence.

An eerie whisper seemed to hover just above their heads. Although their panic had subsided slightly, they were still tense, their hearts pounding in their chests. They moved forward together, but with each step ahead, it became darker and darker.

In the script that they were reading, it was said that children no longer cared to learn about mysterious legends and long-lost civilizations that once called the island home. These civilizations had become lost to time. The allure of exploring the fantastic jungle, with its hidden secrets and thrilling adventures, had lost its appeal to the younger generation. Most kids these days were captivated by technology, lamented the writer of the script, their eyeballs glued to their phone screens, and their adventurous souls stolen. The crying they had heard in the cave was the voice of the island, crying in pain, sad it had been forgotten.

Having finished reading the script, the three friends finally understood that preserving history and culture is essential for future generations. Upon their collective realization of this, the sound of the crying stopped. The trio were now determined to bring the enchanting tales of their ancestors back to life, and they decided to leave the familiar world of technology behind, at least for now.

CAPÍTULO 10

SEGUNDA PARTE: EL GRITO LÚGUBRE EN LAS RUINAS OCULTAS

La noche quiere caer, pero no puede, igual que sus cuerpos quieren parar pero no pueden debido a sus curiosos cerebros que les mantienen en marcha.

Cuando se dirigían a su barco para abandonar la isla, se encontraron con una gran cueva. Curiosos como siempre, decidieron entrar.

Una vez dentro, descubren una serie de grandes cámaras, todas ellas en direcciones diferentes. Para decidir en qué cámara entrar, jugaron al "pito, pito, pito". Así llegaron a la cámara situada más a la izquierda de la cueva.

Mientras recorrían la cámara, descubrieron una antigua escritura. Mientras intentaban descifrar la escritura, de repente, oyeron una voz afligida y llorosa. Miraron arriba y abajo por la cámara, pero no vieron nada. Sus cuerpos empezaron a temblar de miedo. A Pollo se le erizaron los pelos y, tal vez por primera vez en su vida, ¡de repente no tuvo sueño! Marto saltó involuntariamente, haciendo que sus gafas saltasen de su nariz y se rompiesen en el suelo de la cueva (afortunadamente, nunca salía de casa sin un repuesto).

"H-e-ll-o, ¿hay alguien ahí?", gritó Katta con valentía. Todos se detuvieron un momento, pero no hubo respuesta.

"¿H-E-E-LL-o-o?". tartamudeó Pollo, esforzándose por articular bien la palabra.

"¡Shhh!" susurró Katta con urgencia.

"¡No, tú shhh! Mandona", replicó Pollo enfadado.

"Bueno, ya está bien, siempre os estáis peleando como perros y gatos", declaró Marto impaciente. "Voy a caminar más adelante a ver qué puedo averiguar. Vosotros dos esperad aquí".

Antes de que Pollo y Katta pudieran protestar, la cueva quedó repentinamente en silencio. Demasiado silenciosa. Incluso el sonido del agua que goteaba por el borde de las paredes de la cueva había cesado aparentemente.

Silencio total.

Un inquietante susurro parecía flotar justo por encima de sus cabezas. Aunque el pánico había disminuido ligeramente, seguían tensos, con el corazón latiéndoles con fuerza en el pecho. Avanzaron juntos, pero a cada paso que daban se hacía más y más oscuro.

En el guión que estaban leyendo, se decía que los niños ya no se preocupaban por aprender sobre leyendas misteriosas y civilizaciones desaparecidas que una vez llamaron "hogar" a la isla. Estas civilizaciones se habían perdido en el tiempo. El encanto de explorar la asombrosa selva, con sus secretos ocultos y sus emocionantes aventuras, había perdido su atractivo para las nuevas generaciones. La mayoría de los niños de hoy en día estaban cautivados por la tecnología, se lamentaba el guionista, con los ojos pegados a las pantallas de sus teléfonos y el alma aventurera robada. El llanto que habían oído en la cueva era la voz de la isla, que lloraba de dolor, triste por haber sido olvidada.

Al terminar de leer el guión, los tres amigos comprendieron por fin que preservar la historia y la cultura es esencial para las generaciones futuras. Al darse cuenta de ello, el llanto cesó. El trío estaba ahora decidido a devolver a la vida las encantadoras historias de sus antepasados, y deciden dejar atrás el familiar mundo de la tecnología, al menos por ahora.

CHAPTER 11

THE SPARKLE CRYSTAL CAVE

Having now emerged from the chamber of the cave, the trio continued along their journey. At some point along their journey, Katta, Marto, and Pollo stumbled upon yet another cave, but this new cave was quite different.

Entering the cave, the trio were awed as it twinkled with dazzling crystals and gemstones that glittered like a disco ball. They tiptoed inside and met magical creatures guarding various treasures. These creatures were guardians of the island, and they were charmed by the trio's knowledge and respect of the island's history. Because of this, they decided to share the crystal power of the cave with the trio. They learned to use the energy for good and pinky-promised to be responsible. To keep Pollo awake, they played a "Crystal Catch" game using some glowing gems they pried off the walls of the cave. They discovered that with big power comes bigger responsibilities—and lots of sparkles!

CAPÍTULO 11

LA CUEVA DE CRISTAL CENTELLEANTE

Tras salir de la cámara de la cueva, el trío continuó su viaje. En algún punto de su viaje, Katta, Marto y Pollo tropezaron con otra cueva, pero esta nueva cueva era bastante diferente.

Al entrar en la cueva, el trío quedó asombrado al ver cómo centelleaban los deslumbrantes cristales y piedras preciosas, que brillaban como una bola de discoteca. Entraron de puntillas y se encontraron con criaturas mágicas que custodiaban varios tesoros. Estas criaturas eran los guardianes de la isla, y quedaron encantados por los conocimientos y el respeto del trío hacia la historia de la isla. Por ello, decidieron compartir el poder del cristal de la cueva con el trío. Aprendieron a utilizar la energía para el bien y se comprometieron a ser responsables.

Para mantener despierto a Pollo, jugaron a "Atrapar cristales" con unas gemas brillantes que arrancaron de las paredes de la cueva. Descubrieron que un gran poder conlleva una gran responsabilidad, ¡y muchos destellos!

CHAPTER 12

THE MYSTERIOUS JIGGY HEALING GARDEN

Next, they journeyed to the far side of the unfamiliar northern regions in search of a mysterious garden that was rumored to have powerful healing abilities. The trio was a little sore from their trip, and Marto had come down with a case of the sniffles, so they decided to pay it a visit.

As they proceeded along their journey, with just spirit and faith guiding them, they encountered friendly, chatty mosquitos and crazy bees. These strange insects gave some tips on a shortcut they could take to the garden so they could make it there before nightfall. The friends were so grateful for their kind advice, and they continued their way.

Just as dusk was about to fall, the trio discovered the garden. It was just as they imagined, blooming with humongous, rainbow-colored flowers and herbs.

Some were large, and some were small.

Some were red, others blue. Some were still, while others swayed. There was so much diversity among the flowers; it seemed like no two looked (or behaved) the same way.

All this variety seemed to give the garden a supernatural amount of energy. It almost reminded the group of themselves; they all looked and even behaved so differently, but when they were together, there was no challenge they couldn't face.

The friends, glancing around the garden, also noticed that some of the plants and herbs even had wings! They were flying over the garden, sometimes landing and planting themselves for a bit, before deciding to fly off to another part of the garden.

The plants and herbs were very friendly. They approached the group and used their powers to quickly and gently heal them. While they performed their healing magic, their aromatic scents and powerful healing oxygen flowed around the group, uplifting their spirits and giving them energy.

Benevolently, the generous garden offered them a place to stay for as long as they wanted, and it offered them food enough food to cure their hunger, which now felt insatiable. The trio accepted the generous hospitality, and they ate until they had to force themselves to stop!

As night fell on the garden, the group roamed around, listening to the herbs and plants tell their tales and learning about the history of the garden.

The chatty plants wouldn't take a break from talking, and Katta seemingly wouldn't take a break from farting! But at least this time, they didn't smell.

"Your farts stink less than usual," observed Marto, cautiously,

"Grandma said that if you brush your teeth, you will never have a stinky fart," Katta replied, smiling comically and showing off her pearly white teeth.

To keep Pollo energetic, they gave him a magical particular plant that filled him with pep and endless giggles. They learned that every plant and herb in the garden, big or small, was critical and played a role in the community. Whether it swayed or was still, big or small, or red or blue, each plant in the garden was just as important as the one next to it.

CAPÍTULO 12

EL MISTERIOSO JARDÍN CURATIVO DE JIGGY.

A continuación, viajaron hasta el otro extremo de las desconocidas regiones septentrionales en busca de un misterioso jardín del que se rumoreaba que tenía poderosas habilidades curativas. El trío estaba un poco dolorido por el viaje y Marto se había resfriado, así que decidieron visitarlo.

A medida que avanzaban en su viaje, guiados sólo por el espíritu y la fe, se encontraron con mosquitos amistosos y parlanchines y abejas locas. Estos extraños insectos les dieron algunos consejos sobre un atajo que podían tomar para llegar al jardín antes de que anocheciera. Los amigos agradecieron mucho sus amables consejos y continuaron su camino.

Justo cuando estaba a punto de anochecer, el trío descubrió el jardín. Era tal y como lo habían imaginado: floreciente, con flores y hierbas enormes y de los colores del arco iris. Algunas eran grandes, otras pequeñas. Algunas eran rojas, otras azules. Algunas estaban quietas, mientras que otras se balanceaban. Había tanta diversidad entre las flores que parecía que no había dos con el mismo aspecto (o comportamiento).

Toda esta variedad parece dotar al jardín de una energía sobrenatural. Al grupo casi le recuerda a ellos mismos: todos tienen un aspecto y un comportamiento muy diferentes, pero cuando están juntos, no hay reto al que no puedan enfrentarse.

Los amigos también observaron que algunas plantas y hierbas tenían alas. Volaban sobre el jardín, a veces aterrizaban y se plantaban un rato, antes de decidir volar a otra parte del jardín.

Los planes y las hierbas eran muy amistosos. Se acercaron al grupo y utilizaron sus poderes para curarlos rápida y suavemente. Mientras realizaban su magia curativa, sus olores aromáticos y su poderoso oxígeno curativo fluían alrededor del grupo, levantando sus espíritus y dándoles energía.

Benévolamente, el generoso jardín les ofreció un lugar donde quedarse todo el tiempo que quisieran, y les ofreció comida suficiente para curar su hambre, que ahora se sentía insaciable. El trío aceptó la generosa hospitalidad, y comieron hasta que tuvieron que obligarse a parar.

Cuando la noche cayó sobre el jardín, el grupo deambuló por los alrededores, escuchando a las hierbas y plantas contar sus historias y aprendiendo sobre la historia del jardín.

Las plantas parlanchinas no paraban de hablar, y Katta parecía no parar de tirarse pedos. Pero al menos esta vez no olían.

"Tus pedos apestan menos que de costumbre", observó Marto, con cautela,

"La abuela dijo que si te cepillas los dientes, nunca tendrás un pedo apestoso", respondió Katta, sonriendo cómicamente y mostrando sus dientes blancos como perlas.

Para mantener a Pollo con energía, le dieron una planta mágica especial que lo llenaba de ánimo y de risitas interminables. Aprendieron que todas las plantas y hierbas del jardín, grandes o pequeñas, eran importantes y desempeñaban un papel en la comunidad. Tanto si se balanceaba como si estaba quieta, o era grande o pequeña, o roja o azul, cada planta del jardín era tan importante como la de al lado.

All the kids are very useful and clever.
If your parents can't see that, forgive them. Papy and Mamy are sometimes busy, and if there is no one? know that."All kids are a gift to the world. There is not an EXCEPTION.

Each kid in the world has something unique to offer to the world.

CHAPTER 13

THE SKY-HIGH KINGDOM OF COOPERATION AND APPRECIATION

The three departed the garden, more energetic than ever, and with a bit of help from the magical crystals given to them earlier by the cave guardians, they flew up into the clouds to a mystical floating kingdom. It was the first time Pollo managed to stay awake on his own. He was wide-eyed and fascinated by the cloudy skies and the wobbly, floating structures that made up the kingdom. They were greeted and welcomed by the Sky Kingdom's inhabitants, who shared wisdom and knowledge about the sky's role in the earthy world and how the sky was magically interconnected with Mother Earth.

The trio learned from the kingdom's inhabitants that every part of the world, even the tiniest raindrop, plays a role in maintaining sustaining life on Earth. They also learned that cooperation and unity are essential for a happy, harmonious world. The trio suddenly interrupted...

The inhabitants explained that Mother Earth was like an artist who worked for free, doodling the clouds in the sky, carving mountains like giant sandcastles, and teaching birds to sing their songs. She draws sunrises and sunsets, gives us the gifts of water and rain, and creates the stars and moon in the sky. Mother Earth never sends a bill and doesn't ask for anything in return. However, that doesn't mean she doesn't appreciate a "thank you" now and then... To show appreciation, we can try our best to keep our water clean, throw away our garbage, recycle what we can, and try to live in a way that keeps Earth sustainable for future generations.

The trio understood and collectively decided to do their part from now on to keep the Earth clean. Without forgetting that nature, like all children, is also a gift to the world.

CAPÍTULO 13

EL REINO CELESTIAL DE LA COOPERACIÓN Y EL APRECIO

Los tres salieron del jardín, con más energía que nunca, y con un poco de ayuda de los cristales mágicos que les habían dado antes los guardianes de la cueva, volaron hacia las nubes, a un reino mágico flotante. Era la primera vez que Pollo conseguía mantenerse despierto por sí solo. Estaba fascinado por el cielo nublado y las estructuras flotantes que formaban el reino. Fueron recibidos y acogidos por los habitantes del Reino del Cielo, que compartieron con ellos sabiduría y conocimientos sobre el papel del cielo en el mundo terrenal, y sobre cómo el cielo estaba mágicamente interconectado con la Madre Tierra.

El trío aprendió de los habitantes del reino que cada parte del mundo, incluso la gota de lluvia más pequeña, desempeña un papel en el mantenimiento de la vida en la Tierra. También aprendieron que la cooperación y la unidad son esenciales para un mundo feliz y armonioso. El trío interrumpió de repente...

Los habitantes explicaron que la Madre Tierra era como una artista que trabajaba gratis, garabateando las nubes en el cielo, esculpiendo montañas como gigantescos castillos de arena y enseñando a los pájaros a cantar sus canciones. Dibuja amaneceres y atardeceres, nos regala el agua y la lluvia, y crea las estrellas y la luna en el cielo. La Madre Tierra nunca pasa factura y no pide nada a cambio. Sin embargo, eso no significa que no aprecie un "gracias" de vez en cuando... Para demostrar nuestro agradecimiento, podemos hacer todo lo posible por mantener limpia el agua, tirar la basura, reciclar lo que podamos e intentar vivir de forma que la Tierra siga siendo sostenible para las generaciones futuras.

El trío lo entendió y decidió colectivamente poner de su parte a partir de ahora para mantener limpia la Tierra, Sin olvidar, que la naturaleza como los niños son también un regalo para el mundo.

CHAPTER 14

THE FANTABULOUS FRIENDSHIP FINALE

Upon completing their journey, the trio returned home to a village-wide, confetti-filled celebration. To their surprise, they found all the magical friends that they met along their journey waiting for them! The adventure not only brought them closer together, but taught them many important lessons about the importance of diversity and the power of unity, cooperation, and friendship. Not to mention that magic seemed to be hidden in every corner of the world and within each and every human being.! They also learned that they could lean on each other when times were tough.

Grateful and beaming with joy, they vowed to keep exploring and sharing their wisdom with the community. And guess what? Pollo stayed awake for the entire celebration, thanks to the lessons and support from his friends and the enchanting creatures they met during their whimsical escapades.

"Morto, Pollo and Katta's journeys will continue..."

Wait! Don't go yet, there are more gifts for you. "AFFIRMATIONS" But first...

If you enjoyed this crunchy but captivating adventure, LET YOUR **SOUL** SHARE YOUR EXPERIENCE IN A REVIEW. — It will mean the world for me and others. Thank you.

As well, if you want to GIVE A SMILE to OTHER KIDS, SHARE". And If you want to read more stories like this one, SUBSCRIBE to my newsletter or follow me on social media to find out what's new.

Until another time of many SMILES-filled with love, with your favorite storyteller; take care, and thank you again. **Love ya.** — Angelica Rockford.

CAPÍTULO 14

EL FANTABULOSO FINAL DE LA AMISTAD

Tras completar su viaje, el trío regresó a casa en medio de una celebración llena de bienvenida por todo el pueblo. Para su sorpresa, ¡encontraron a todos los amigos mágicos que habían conocido a lo largo del viaje esperándoles!

La aventura no sólo les unió más, sino que les enseñó muchas lecciones importantes sobre la importancia de la diversidad y el poder de la unidad, la cooperación y la amistad. Por no hablar de que la magia parecía esconderse en todos los rincones del mundo y en el interior de cada uno de los humanos. También aprendieron que podían apoyarse los unos en los otros en los momentos difíciles.

Agradecidos y radiantes de alegría, prometieron seguir explorando y compartiendo su sabiduría con la comunidad. ¿Y adivina qué? Pollo permaneció despierto durante toda la celebración, gracias a las lecciones y al apoyo de sus amigos y de las encantadoras criaturas que conocieron durante sus caprichosas escapadas.

"Los viajes de Morto, Pollo y Katta Continuarán...".

¡Espera! No te vayas todavía, hay más regalos para ti. "AFIRMACIONES" Pero primero...

Si has disfrutado de esta crujiente pero cautivadora aventura DEJA QUE TU ALMA ESCRIBA to experiencia en un **(Review)"** Significara el mundo para mi y para otros.

Así como, si quieres DONAR UNA SONRISA a OTROS NIÑOS, COMPARTE". Si quieres leer más historias como esta, SUSCRÍBETE a mi boletín o sígueme en las redes sociales para enterarte de las novedades.

Hasta otro dia, lleno de SONRISA con tu author favorito, cuídate y gracias de nuevo. **Te quiero.** - Angélica Rockford.

REVIEW

Dear Reader

"This is another amazing book, adding to the wealth of mesmerizing works out there, where EACH stands on its own UNIQUE essence and purity."

I want to, "thank you" personally for your support to all authors and the support for helping your infant's soul and yourself to "remember who you always were"—LOVE. "The sleepy head and the three wishes," for me, is a world of laughter" I hope you and your infant had a lot of giggly moments together and a deeper connection between both.

As an author, feedback from readers like you also opens doors for others to enjoy a laugh too. Insights not only help me to improve as a writer but also helps other readers discover the book and benefit themselves as human beings from this creativity or even decide if it's right for them.

To leave a review on Amazon, simply go to the book's page and click on the "Write a customer review" button. I would be thrilled to hear your thoughts on the book and appreciate any feedback you may have.

Thank you again for your support and for choosing to share this adventure with me. I hope you enjoyed the book, and I look forward to hearing from you soon.

Best regards, Angelica Rockford
Instagram @nawe_illustrator —Our Brilliant! ILLUSTRATOR
Instagram @angelicarockford —The Author
Instagram @sunkullaybooks—The Brand
Twitter@sunkullaybooks —The brand and the Author
TikTok   @angelicarockford @sunkullay
Facebook @sunkullay & Angelica Rockford.

About the Confidence Bonus

Your opinion about your child influences their behavior and their ENTIRE life—Angelica Rockford. ∞...

Moving to a new country without knowing the language can be a daunting experience for both adults and children. I've seen children struggle with fear when their parents abruptly decide to relocate. There is often no place for debate with conventional parents. All parental decisions are expected to be met with a simple "YES!" from children. Parents may need to realize the enormous emotional and psychological impact such a relocation can have on their child, mainly if they are not mentally prepared.

The language barrier can be a considerable hurdle upon arrival in a new place, especially when it comes to making friends. Building friendships becomes much more difficult for a child who already struggles with poor self-esteem and feelings of insecurity. Unfortunately, these flaws can sometimes lead to them being targeted by bullies. In severe circumstances, such events can cast a long shadow over a child's childhood, causing permanent trauma. So, how can we address this issue? The crucial word here is CONFIDENCE. But what exactly is confidence?

Confidence is feeling safe being you. Confidence is the belief in oneself, the conviction that one can handle challenges even when confronted with unfamiliar or difficult situations. It's not just about keeping an upright posture, though that can help kids. Confidence goes more profound; it is rooted in mindset. It includes love, acknowledgment, and, most importantly, self-trust. If you provide them with three essential elements at home: love, security, and attention, you will lay a solid foundation for their confidence.

Confidence is essential for emotional development. When I say "love," I'm referring to those critical moments when your child makes a mistake. It does not entail berating them or casting doubt on their abilities with comments like, "Why can't you do anything right?" or "Why do you always mess up?" Instead of being loving, such statements imply to the child that they are inadequate or unworthy. I speak from experience; as a child, I felt the same way every time I heard such criticisms. Instead, imagine if every mistake was met with encouragement: "Good job! You'll do even better the next day. It's okay to make mistakes; you're still getting used to your surroundings. Everyone learns in small steps." What would your child's reaction be? They would undoubtedly come to trust you. Undoubtedly, they'd grow to trust you even more, seeing you not just as a parent but also as a confidante and friend.

Begin by showering your child with positive, affirming, and courageous words for any achievement, no matter how minor. These expressions of love and affirmation help to boost their confidence. You are the one they most want to hear those encouraging words from. You are nothing short of a hero in their eyes. It's not just about noticing their mistakes; it's also about celebrating their successes. In simple words: *Don't be good just seeing the wrong things, but also the good things they do. Then, see yourself in the same way.* We frequently need to begin our healing journey before becoming parents or during our parenting years. The way we regard ourselves reflects how we treat our children.

Because of this understanding, I've included powerful affirmations explicitly tailored for you and your child. These are intended to strengthen your bond, ensuring a memorable childhood filled with cherished memories.

Your child will remember these special times with you for the rest of his or her life. They'll be proud to have you as their parent, and you'll know you did the right thing by giving them the most valuable gift of all: confidence.

Consider your child, full of confidence, taking on challenges fearlessly and emerging stronger from each setback. Do you ever wonder why your child has these natural abilities? They aren't just gifts; they are founded on faith, which manifests as confidence.

This is the true essence of self-assurance and self-awareness. When children deeply believe in their worth and trust in their inherent abilities, they are prepared to face any challenges in life. And what about making new friends? That process becomes automatic and natural. They operate with love and trust, leaving no room for FEAR.

The good news is that affirmations can play an essential role in their emotional development by increasing their dynamic intelligence through repetition. For example, when you tell your child, "You are loved," or "You are brilliant," they genuinely believe it and see it as a reflection of how you see them. Your words have an impact on their world. The more you repeat these affirmations, the more they will believe in their own brilliance, worthiness, and capability. With each affirmation, you feed their confidence.

You're creating a powerful self-image for them, one that will stay with them for the rest of their lives. It's important to understand, however, that the same is true for negative affirmations and negative *afformations*.

An example of a Negative Affirmation: "You are not good enough (you are not a good kid)."

What are Negative afformations? They are self-defeating inquiries that reinforce negative beliefs. Instead of challenging limiting beliefs, they cause you to question your own worth or abilities negatively.

Negative afformations can be probing questions like "why are you like this" or "why can't you be like your brother, sister, cousin or the other kid on the class." You're basically saying, "Why are you not worthy for me?" "Why are you not the kid I want?" "Why you are not worthy nothing." As previously stated, this communicates to them that they are unimportant...and that causes their self-esteem be low.

According to Noah St. John, afformations go straight to the subconscious mind for answers. That is the reason we have to be careful with affirmations on kids, especially from parents to children, that are often used in harmful comparisons. When you compare two children, it's as if you're asking, "why are you not the same person." This not only dims a child's light when they are compared by their own parents but makes them hate themselves as they cannot satisfy their parents by being themselves. You're essentially programming limitations into their mind, making them feel inadequate and instilling fear.

Change your perspective. Remember no two people are alike, not even siblings. Every child is distinct. How would you like your son to remember you when he grows up? Not only will your words help him or are they only destroying him. Ask yourself that question. Consider your own childhood: is there any hurtful remark from a parent that you remember? Consider the effect it had on you. So...

Remember that other people's opinions, especially yours as a parent, have a big influence on your child. They can shape their behavior and influence their entire life journey. As a result, we must choose our words carefully.

Affirmations and Afformations are potent tools when are used in positive ways, that shape a child's perception of reality, guiding them toward confidence, achievement, resilience, help them to cope better, and the foundation of meaningful relationships. Understand that one's thoughts and beliefs are among the most powerful tools he or she possesses. Let's make this journey as bright as it should be! Give them the love and opportunities they deserve by putting their well-being and mental health

we all deserve to be recognized and seen specially from OURSELVES.

BONUS ONE

AFFIRMATIONS FOR CONFIDENCE AND TO MAKE FRIENDS EASILY WITH ANYONE.

We are all lovable...

- I AM GRATEFUL FOR MY HEALTH AND MY LAUGHTER
- I LOVE MYSELF
- I AM CONFIDENT
- I AM KIND
- I AM SAFE
- I LIKE MYSELF

We all are worthy.

— I AM A PRECIOUS SOUL, SHINING BRIGHTLY WITH MY UNIQUE SPARKLE. I LOVE MYSELF.

— I AM A JOYFUL AND ENCHANTMENT SONG, FILLING THE AIR WITH MY BEAUTIFUL MELODY. I AM LOVABLE.

— I AM GRATEFUL TO MY MOMMY AND DADDY FOR TAKING CARE OF ME (WONDERFUL PEOPLE WHO TAKE CARE OF ME (IF APPLY))

—I AM VERY PATIENT WITH MYSELF WHEN I DO MISTAKES, AND I REMEMBER THAT "I AM NOT MY MISTAKES" AND IT IS OK TO MAKE MISTAKES, I DOING A GREAT JOY, I LEARNING, AND I GROWING. I LOVE MYSELF.

—I HAVE COMPASSION FOR MYSELF ON MY WEAK DAYS; THOSE DAYS WHEN I FEEL SAD, ANGRY, OR NOT UNDERSTOOD, I GIVE MYSELF TONS OF LOVE, TOLERANCE, AND CARE, AND I TELL MYSELF."

—I AM NOT MY UNLOVING THOUGHTS

—I AM NOT MY UNKIND WONDERS, I AM NOT MY FEARS

—I AM LEARNING TO EXPRESS AND COMMUNICATE MY FEELINGS BETTER SO OTHERS CAN UNDERSTAND ME BETTER.

we all are important

we all matter. We all are unique.

—I AM KIND TO MYSELF.

—I FORGIVE EASILY BECAUSE EVERYBODY IS ALLOWED TO MAKE MISTAKES, INCLUDING MYSELF...

—FORGIVING IS A GIFT TO MYSELF. IT HELPS MY HEART'S HOUSE TO BE HAPPY AND LIGHT WITHOUT LETTING HEAVY ENERGY COME INSIDE.

—I AM LOVABLE, WORTHY, AND WONDERFUL, LIKE THE SUN AND THE SKY

-I LIKE MYSELF

Hey...buddy...! pay attention to your affirmations.

— I AM A HAPPY LITTLE CLOUD FLOATING THROUGH THE SKY WITH A MAGIC SMILE BECAUSE I AM ALIVE.

— I AM NEVER ALONE; I ALWAYS HAVE A POWERFUL SPIRIT INSIDE ME THAT I CAN RELY ON AND TRUST! WHEN I NEED A GUIDE.

— I AM A COLORFUL ARCH, BRINGING JOY, PEACE, AND HOPE AFTER EACH STORM.

— I SWEETEN THE EXISTENCE OF EVERYONE AROUND ME.

All kids are beautiful

— I AM THE LIGHT OF MY FAMILY AND EVERYONE AROUND ME BECAUSE I SPREAD JOY AND HAPPINESS WHEREVER I GO.

— I AM A GENIUS, ALWAYS LEARNING AND GROWING BRIGHTER.

— I APPRECIATE MOMMY AND DADDY'S ATTENTION AND LOVE FOR MAKING ME FEEL IMPORTANT.

All the kids are very useful and clever.
If your parents can't see that, forgive them. Papy and Mamy are sometimes busy, and if there is no one? know that."All kids are a gift to the world. There is not an EXCEPTION.

All kids are smart...

— I AM GRATEFUL FOR MY BODY, MY MIND, AND MY HEART.

— I AM A BEAUTIFUL BUTTERFLY, TRANSFORMING AND GROWING EVERY DAY.

— I LOVE MYSELF BECAUSE I AM BRILLIANT

— I AM A BRAVE EXPLORER, READY TO FACE ANY ADVENTURE WITH COURAGE AND TRUST.

— I AM LOVABLE, I AM WORTHY, I AM BEAUTIFUL, LIKE THE SUN AND THE SKY.

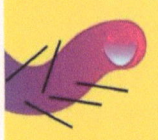

—MY HEART IS FILLED WITH LOVE, KINDNESS, AND FORGIVENESS.

—I AM GRATEFUL FOR MY EXISTENCE.

—I AM A CREATIVE SPIRIT, CONSTANTLY DISCOVERING NEW WAYS TO EXPRESS MYSELF. LIKE WHEN I AM ANGRY OR NOT FEELING WELL.

—I AM LIKABLE BECAUSE I AM KIND, FRIENDLY, AND LOVING (BOY)/(GIRL.)

All kids are gifted, and their gifts are often different, some discover early, and others will discover later. But All kids are brilliant!!

— I DON'T HOLD GRUDGES OR ANY NEGATIVE ENERGY; I GIVE UP EASILY NON-LOVING THOUGHTS.

All kids have a powerful hero and a magic princess inside them.

- I FORGIVE EASILY AND FAST; I LET IT GO. I FOCUS ON MY EXCELLENT SPARKLING ENERGY.

— I AM BRILLIANT LIKE EVERYONE, AND I HAVE MY UNIQUE TALENTS

— I AM A GOOD LISTENER AND A CARING FRIEND TO EVERYONE AND INCLUDING MYSELF.

- I'M A SUNSHINE SUPERHERO THAT SPREADS JOY WHEREVER I GO!
- I'M A DARING ADVENTURER WHO EXPLORES THE WORLD WITH ZEAL AND PASSION!

- MY HEART IS LIKE A GIGANTIC GENIE FOR EVERYONE, FULL OF LOVE AND KINDNESS!

- I'M AN EXTREMELY IMAGINATIVE YOUNGSTER WHO COMES UP WITH AMAZING METHODS TO HAVE FUN!

- I LIVE IN THE PRESENT!
- MY FUN IS ALWAYS IN THE PRESENT, NOT IN THE YESTERDAY, NOT EVEN IN THE TOMORROW BUT IN THE NOW
- I CHOOSE TO HAVE FUN NOW..........

Hola, como estas!..Aloja

- I'M A LISTENING WIZARD WHO MAKES PEOPLE FEEL HEARD AND CARED FOR, INCLUDING MYSELF!

- I'M A CHEERFUL, BOUNCY BALL FULL OF JOY AND LEARNING!

- I'M LIKE A BUTTERFLY, EVOLVING INTO SOMETHING SPECTACULAR!

- I'M A WISE LITTLE BEING WHO IS CONSTANTLY LEARNING AND GROWING SMARTER!

- MY IMAGINATION IS A MAGNIFICENT TREASURE BOX FULL OF NEVER-ENDING DELIGHTS!

Time to connect with papa, mama or any kind of family.

- "I'M A SUPERHERO OF KINDNESS, AND I USE MY ABILITIES TO HELP OTHERS AND MAKE THE WORLD A BETTER PLACE!

- "I AM THE BOSS OF MY MIND; I WATCH MY THOUGHTS; I LET THEM COME AND GO. I REMEMBER THAT WITHOUT MY ATTENTION, THEY DON'T HAVE POWER!!.

- "EACH BREATH IS LIKE A LITTLE SPA VACATION FOR MY FEELINGS. I RELEASE NO-LOVING THOUGHTS NOW, AND I INHALE LOVE!"

- "MY SADNESS IS LIKE A CLOUD; SOMETIMES IT RAINS, BUT THEN IT MOVES ON. SUNSHINE, HERE WE COME!"

- "I GIVE MY FEELINGS A VIP TOUR OF MY MIND, WITH NO CRITICISM ACTING AS THE TOUR GUIDE."

All kids always do things RIGHT. They are learning—one step at a time.

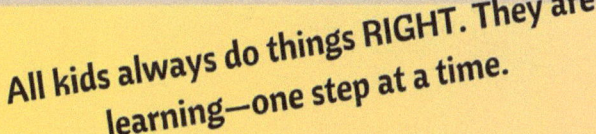

-"SORRY, SADNESS, YOU'RE JUST A VISITOR. THANKS FOR STOPPING BY, BUT IT'S TIME TO SAY GOODBYE BECAUSE NOW I AM GOING TO START TO DANCE AND FEEL GOOD.

-"I'M THE EYE OF THE HURRICANE, WATCHING THE WINDS BUT STAYING PEACEFUL."

-"MY ANGER IS LIKE A CATERPILLAR. WITH A LITTLE TIME AND MINDFULNESS, IT BECOMES AN UNDERSTANDING BUTTERFLY."

-"MY THOUGHTS PLAY OUT LIKE A MOVIE." I WATCH THEM, APPRECIATE THE PLOT, BUT KEEP IN MIND THAT IT'S JUST A SHOW."

All kids have a soul and a friend inside them.

All kids are lovable by simply existing.

- I KNOW MY FEELINGS ARE MY FRIENDS. THEY TELL ME WHEN I'M PLEASED, SAD, TERRIFIED, OR ANGRY. WHEN I EXPERIENCE THESE THINGS, I TRY TO FIGURE OUT WHY. THIS ALLOWS ME TO EXPRESS MY SENTIMENTS TO OTHERS.

- I RESPOND, NOT REACT. THE DJ AT MY PARTY IS NOT MY EMOTIONS, BUT UNDERSTANDING MY FEELINGS. I CHOOSE TO SEE THINGS DIFFERENTLY.

- EVERY BREATH IS A MAGIC TRICK THAT BRINGS ME PEACE BY DISSOLVING MY ANGER.

—I am a kind (girl)/(boy)

—MY IMAGINATION IS A MAGICAL WORLD FILLED WITH ENDLESS POSSIBILITIES.

Each kid in the world has something unique to offer to the world.

—I AM A SUPERHERO, USING MY POWERS FOR GOOD AND HELPING OTHERS.

—I AM A CUDDLY TEDDY BEAR, ALWAYS READY TO GIVE AND RECEIVE HUGS. I LOVE BEING MYSELF

—I AM A SHINING STAR, LIGHTING UP THE SKY WITH MY BRILLIANCE AND BEAUTY.

—THANK YOU FOR FOOD, THANK YOU FOR A ROUGH OVER MY HEAD, THANK YOU FOR SWEATS, AND ALL THE BLESSINGS FROM UNIVERSE.

—I AM A GENTLE BREEZE FLOWING THROUGH LIFE GRACEFULLY AND EASILY.

—I AM A BLOOMING FLOWER / OAK TREE, SPREADING BEAUTY AND CHARM TO THE EYES OF OTHERS.

Ho..Yes, thanks to you to Papa and Mami for everything they do for you.

All kids in the world are a GIFT of happiness.

"I am a perfect child of the universe; I am mind, I can think, I can choose, my mind is powerful, and my value is immeasurable."

"Every moment is a new opportunity for love, growth, and understanding."

"I am connected to an endless source of strength and love."

"Miracles happen in my life every day, reminding me of the beauty within and around me."

"I am so thankful for my mind. All bodies may be limited, but my mind is unlimited and kind.
"Love and Unity" is my nature. We are all one.

I am powerful and lovable.

"I love myself."
"Loving myself is healing myself."
"Loving myself is being my best friend."

Ho, Yes! A new country. A new adventure to explore.!

"I am brave for embracing new adventures and beginnings."

"Every day, I grow stronger in my new environment."

"My cultural roots make me unique and add richness to this new place."

"I am capable of building bridges between my past and my future."

"My superpower is being different; it allows me to see the world in vibrant colors."

—I AM A MIGHTY POWERFUL MOUNTAIN, STANDING FIRM AND STEADY NO MATTER WHAT COMES MY WAY. I AM READY TO LEARN AND SUCCEED.!

—I AM A RIVER OF PURE LOVE, FLOWING THROUGH THE WORLD AND TOUCHING THE HEARTS OF OTHERS.

—I AM PROUD OF MYSELF AND THE HUMAN BEING I AM BECOMING. I LOVE MYSELF AND OTHERS.

French: Salut, petit chat!" (Hello, little kitty!)

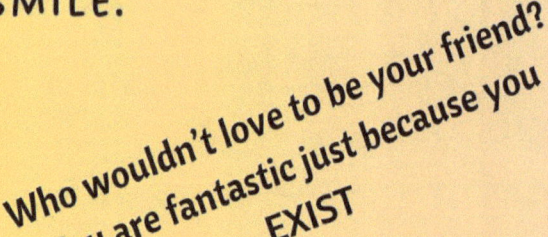

— MAKING FRIENDS IS EASY

— BEING MY FRIEND IS EASY

— FEELING CONFIDENT IS NATURAL

— I AM CONFIDENT; I FEEL CONFIDENT

— I WALK TALL, SECURE WITH A SERENE FRONT, FRIENDLY-RESTED EYES, AND A WARM SMILE.

- I AM WORTHY

- I MATTER

- I BELIEVE IN WHOM I AM

- I AM KIND TO MYSELF

- I AM COMPASSIONATE WITH MYSELF EACH TIME THINGS DON'T GO MY WAY

- I AM PATIENT WITH OTHERS WHEN THEY ARE NOT FEELING WELL.

Who wouldn't love to be your friend? You are fantastic just because you EXIST

— FORGIVENESS IS PEACE

— I FORGIVE EASILY

— I AM FORGIVENESS

— I AM APPRECIATION

— I AM THE PRESENT; I AM NOT THE PAST

— I RELEASE THE PAST, I FORGIVE THE PAST, I AM FREE FROM THE PAST

— I WALK TALL, SECURE WITH A SERENE FRONT, FRIENDLY-RESTED EYES, AND A WARM SMILE.

- I AM WORTHY

- I MATTER; I DESERVE TO BE SEEN, APPRECIATED, AND LOVED

- I BELIEVE IN WHOM I AM

- I AM KIND TO MYSELF

- I AM COMPASSIONATE WITH MYSELF EACH TIME THINGS DON'T GO MY WAY

- I AM PATIENT WITH OTHERS WHEN THEY ARE NOT FEELING WELL.

_Forgiveness is a gift of peace...

—I HAVE THE RIGHT TO SAY "NO"

—OTHERS HAVE THE RIGHT TO SAY "NO," WITHOUT ME GETTING UPSET.

—I HAVE THE RIGHT TO CHANGE MY MIND, EVEN AT THE LAST MINUTE.

—OTHERS HAVE THE RIGHT TO CHANGE THEIR MIND EVEN AT THE LAST MINUTE, WITHOUT ME GETTING UPSET.

—HEALTHY BOUNDARIES PROTECT MY EMOTIONS

—RESPECTING MYSELF IS LOVING MYSELF

—LOVING MYSELF IS HEALING

—RESPECTING OTHERS IS LOVING THEM AS THEY ARE.

—I RESPECT THE BOUNDARIES OF OTHERS.

—ASSUMING IT IS A LIE, I BETTER ASK FOR CLARITY AND UNDERSTANDING

—I ACCEPT MYSELF, I ACCEPT OTHERS

—I EMBRACE MY IMPERFECTIONS; I EMBRACE THE IMPERFECTION OF OTHERS.

—I AM HUMBLE   I am kind and You are kind
—I RESPECT MY DECISIONS
—EACH TIME I FORGIVE MYSELF, I GET CLOSER TO MYSELF, AND THE CLOSER I GET, THE CLOSER I GET TO MY FATHER, "GOD."
—EACH TIME I FORGIVE OTHERS, I GET CLOSER TO THEM, WHICH GETS ME CLOSER TO THE UNIVERSE.
—I NEVER FORCE MYSELF TO DO SOMETHING I DON'T WANT.

—BEFORE FORGIVENESS, I UNDERSTAND MY PERCEPTIONS AND WHAT I SEE. FORGIVENESS IS NOT FORCING MYSELF TO DO SOMETHING I AM NOT READY TO DO. I AM PATIENT, CAN WAIT UNTIL I UNDERSTAND THE SITUATION CLEARLY, AND AM READY TO FORGIVE!!!
—EVERYTHING IS FINE RIGHT NOW, RIGHT HERE
—I DON'T JUDGE WHAT I DON'T UNDERSTAND DEEPLY
—I DON'T JUDGE MYSELF

"I am lovable and Important"

"I am my best friend."

Those are my superpowers.

"Being grateful is like a magic."

"I am grateful for all the things I have.

"I am my best friend."

"I can do everything because I can think."

I love myself

I trust myself

REVIEW

"Dear reader "

This is another fantastic book, adding to the wealth of mesmerizing works out there, where EVERYONE stands on their own UNIQUE essence and purity.

I want to "thank you" personally for your support to all the authors and the support to help your infant's soul and yourself to "remember who you always were"- LOVE. "The Sleepyhead and the Three Wishes", for me, is a world of laughter" I hope you and your baby have had many moments of laughter together and a deeper connection between the two of you.

As an author, comments from readers like you open doors for others to enjoy a laugh as well. Feedback not only helps me improve as a writer but also helps other readers discover the book and benefit as human beings from this creavity or even decide if it's right for them.

To SHARE YOUR EXPERIENCE IN A REVIEW on Amazon, just go to the book page and click on the "Write a customer review" button. I would love to hear your thoughts on the book and would appreciate any feedback.

Thank you again for your support and for choosing to share r this adventure with me. I hope you enjoyed the book, and I look forward to hearing from you soon. Instagram @nawe¬_illustrator -Illustrator

Instagram @angelicarockford -The author

Twitter & Instagram @sunkullaybooks -The brand (sunkullay and angelica Rockford)

Twi er @sunkullaybooks -The brand and Author

TikTok @angelicarockford @sunkullay

Facebook @sunkullay & Angelica Rockford.

Monjila Akther. Fiver: Layout Design

 @angelicarockford
@sunkullaybooks

  Sunkullay & Angelica Rockford.
@sunkullaybooks

 infosunkullay@gmail.com

Acknowledgments

The journey of a book from a writer's mind to the reader's hands involves many passionate individuals. We are grateful to our illustrator, "Nawanjana Nanayakkara; " Your talent has breathed life and magic into our story. Thank you for filling our pages with charm and our hearts with wonder.

To all who collaborated as part of this process, thanks for your dedication and commitment to bringing this vision to life; I appreciate not only your talents but also your brilliant and generous beings; thanks.

To our cherished readers, young and young-at-heart, this story is a gift for you. Your laughter, imagination, and love for adventure and magic are why stories like this bloom. I wish for this book to nurture your curiosity and create memories between you and that trustworthy person that is vibrant as the illustrations on these pages. Let this book be a mirror that reflects your unique brilliance and a window that opens to a world where everyone is valued and connected, including yourself. A world where making friends becomes easy and natural.

To our loving parents, teachers, and caregivers who are the first heroes in a child's world, thank you for your constant support, patience, and care. This book is an extended hand, a tool to strengthen your bond with your little ones, helping you instill essential life lessons and better manage their emotions, fostering a brighter future and emotional well-being.

Rooted in my service to spread love, laughter, joy, and light through this work and my mission and passion to teach children about life's essential lessons - the things many of us are still learning. I humbly contribute to that ongoing education by celebrating this book on diversity, friendship, teamwork, inclusion, generosity, and unity.

I am also immensely grateful for the sagacity of every mentor I've had and for the unparalleled wisdom that only life's journey can impart. "To Martin Merayo" Jorge Pell Icer" "Louise hay" "Marisa Peer" Buddha and many other incredible teachers.

This book shares what I've learned so far and hints at the lessons still waiting to be explored. So, I thank you for my experiences, particularly those filled with pain and the studies I had to learn the hard way, that form the core of this book. I owe the most profound thanks to these transformative stories they've bestowed upon me.

And lastly, in my journey of reflection and growth, 'A Course in Miracles' has been an unwavering beacon. My heartfelt gratitude goes to the Foundation for Inner Peace for their stewardship of the edition that has profoundly influenced me. Their dedication to this transformative work has been instrumental in shaping the insights shared in this book.

So, let this book be a testament to the power of stories, the magic of childhood, and the joy of learning together and as a cherished companion on your journey of growth and discovery. My heart is full of gratitude for every person, every moment, and every lesson that made this journey possible. Thank you to everyone who contributed to making this vision come to life.

Dedication Of Gratitude

I dedicate this book as a thank you to my brothers and sisters:

Yoni and my little nephew, Jared, Vanesa, Huberth, and Walter Alfonzo. I believe in you and admire you with honor and courage. I respect your strength, resilience, and your ability to embrace adversity, find light in every dark place, and discover hidden treasures in the darkest moments. These are your weapons, and they're what has made YOU the incredible people that you are today. You set the example that your children will follow, allowing them to live life intensely. I applaud and respect all of you for that. To my uncle Oswaldo – I am immensely grateful to you. And to Kevin Madden, I say "Gracias" because, thanks to you, this book is possible.

And finally, thanks to all authors, especially the new ones.

Suppose a new author can't recognize and appreciate that their sacrifice and hard work allowed them to create something with no guarantee it would pay off. In that case, I don't know who else will?

So, a "thank you to me" for not letting me abandon this book, even when I did it more than a billion times, sometimes reaching a point of exhaustion from fighting with many doubts and "what ifs", but persevering anyway. Crying from having so many ideas but seemingly going NOWHERE during these past three years! At points, I almost deleted everything, but still PERSISTING.

Despite all the late nights, you kept showing up every day at your desk to finish this book without being sure it would result in anything. All you had was faith, determination, love, and belief. But the smiles and laughter I saw along the way made it all worth it.

And that's all I wanted. I love you, and I give a deep thanks to that courageous inner voice. Thanks to God for any creative insights I had, the wisdom I gained from each of my experiences, and the lovable ideas that came from Him.

www.ingramcontent.com/pod-product-compliance
Lightning Source LLC
Chambersburg PA
CBHW042246100526
44587CB00002B/41